INDIA'S ENERGY SECURITY AND INDO-US NUCLEAR DEAL

Dr. Nisar Ahmad Meer

India's Energy Security and Indo – US Nuclear Deal

ISBN-13: 978-1508474012

ISBN-10: 150847401X

PUBLISHED BY
CREATESPACE INDEPENDENT PUBLISHING PLATFORM

Publishing Country
INDIA

Date of Publishing
February 2015

TABLE OF CONTENTS

PREFACE

In recent times security is being interpreted increasingly as comprehensive security, the focus has been shifted towards the human security, the economic security as well as environmental security. As defined by the United Nation's Human Development Report of 1994, human security includes safety from chronic threats and harmful disruptions in the patterns of daily life. In the growing literature, the concept of human security has been expanded to include economic, health and environmental concerns for energy security become important.

The European Commission defines energy security as, "the ability to ensure that future essential energy needs can be met, both by means of adequate domestic resources worked under economically acceptable condition or maintained as strategic resources, and by calling up on accessible and stable external sources supplemented appropriately by strategic stocks".

Energy Security and state security are closely interlinked. Energy security plays an important role in the development of country. It enhances a nations economic power and therefore, political status by providing it with the resources to pull its people out of poverty and pursue national growth and development. The Indo- US nuclear agreement all shows case the increasing importance of energy as a driver of national and international politics.

India is among the top four consumers of energy just behind the U.S., China and Japan, India's total primary energy demand in 1997-98 was 25.5 million tons and this is expected to rise up to the 770 million tons in 2020. Currently the share of fuels in primary

energy dominated by coal and oil. India cannot meet this demand domestically and has to rely on outside supplies. This creates a situation of dependence and call for
Cooperation from other nations-states.

Currently energy resources such as coal and oil are becoming extremely depleted and will run out in the near future. The best replacement is the nuclear energy. It is the fastest growing power generation industries in the world, with this regard it is the safest, cleanest and most efficient. Today 15 percent of the world's electricity comes from nuclear power. As for the India's nuclear energy is concerned it is the fourth largest source of electricity. This industry is expected to undergo a significant expansion in the coming years by passing the Indo- US nuclear deal, and then India is expected to generate an additional 25,000mw of nuclear power by 2020.

There has always been acute awareness of the fact that some of the materials technologies and expertise that are relevant for peaceful use of nuclear energy can be used equally for making nuclear weapons. India conduct a nuclear test in 1974 partly in response of external challenges, however, it claimed that the detonation was a peaceful explosion. India did not declare itself to be a nuclear power until it conducted a seemed series of nuclear test in 1998. India also did not sign on NPT and CTBT also due to its external challenges from various countries. Through this reason India facieses number of sanctions many of which were lifted by late 2000 A.D.

The purpose of the (Indo-US Nuclear Deal) agreement is to enable full civil nuclear and energy cooperation between the India and the United States. The agreement provides full civil nuclear energy cooperation covering nuclear reactors and aspects of the associated nuclear fuel cycle including enrichment and reprocessing.

This agreement also opens the doors for cooperation in civil nuclear energy with other countries. This agreement provides for the application of IAEA safeguards to transferred material and equipment.

The present study contains six chapters. The first chapter shows the concept of comprehensive security and also highlights different aspects of security. The second chapter deals with energy security that plays an important role in state security. The third chapter deals with India's Energy Scenario and Politics which shows its various related issues. The fourth chapter deals with Nuclear energy and nuclear proliferation, it shows that how nuclear energy is also used for weapons also. The fifth chapter deals with Indo- US nuclear deal and its role in enhancing India's energy security, through which India can use nuclear energy in peaceful purposes. The sixth and the last chapter deals with assessment of indo-us nuclear deal (123 agreement) in different aspects.

CHAPTER - I
COMPREHENSIVE VIEW OF SECURITY

The term security means freedom from danger a sense of safety or a feeling of assurance. The Latin word, "Securities" means a state of non worry and the Russian word "Benzopasanost", means a state of non danger.

Security is in objective sense, the absence of threats to acquired values and in a subjective sense, the absence of fear that such values will be attacked. Barry Buzan defines, In the case of security, the discussion is in the context of the international system. Security is about the ability of states and societies to maintain their independent identity and their functional integrity.

Barry Buzan, in his study, people state and fear, argues for a view of security which includes political, economic, societal, environmental as well as military aspects and which is also defined in broader international terms. This involves states overcoming excessively self referenced security policies and thinking instead about the security interests of their neighbors. In traditional realism, security is very close to power in its practical significance and international politics like all politics, is a struggle for power,In other words, to be secure a state must have the physical ability to militarily deter attacks and/or repel actual attacks. In effect the predominance of the realist paradigm in international relations led to the meaning of security being subsumed under the rubric of power.

INTRODUCTION

Security has traditionally been defined in terms of states and the qualities of state hood .The modern science of security studies (in the traditional sense), as Steven Walt argues, has evolved around seeking cumulative knowledge. "About the role of military force". Until the end of the cold war, national security as it was known always focused on the military defense the state. In contrast to comprehensive security the traditional concept of national security embraces two distinct characteristics. First, Security is commensurate with national survival in a system of world politics i.e. inherently contentious and anarchical and state is the central unit of analysis,2nd understanding force postures and capabilities is a key tenet of traditional security .Sovereign states develop military doctrines :weapon system serve their defense but may also intensify interstate conflicts and fuel security dilemmas.

The classical view, associated with for instance, Morgenthau (1978) differs from the so called English School variation of Bull& Wight and those who emblemize a groan account of the central role of international society. Realism always include power politics, the balance of power and the politics of territoriality as its central concepts or at least as centers of contention. Realism's state centeredness is extremely pervasive, further more; our emphasis in this project would still be the general realist disposition to reductionism in claiming the autonomy of international politics and its neglect of people and their security in relation to the state. In other words, we can use a general realist position in comparing it with other ways of thinking about security whilst accepting, and being aware of a number of variations.

In traditional realism, security is very close to power in its practical significance and international politics like all politics, is a struggle for power, in other words, to be secure a state must have the physical ability to militarily deter attacks or repel actual attacks. In effect the predominance of the realist paradigm in international relations led to the meaning of security being subsumed under the rubric of power. There is thus a double tragedy in realist security, the first is that it is historical, this means that the laws of realism are said to be scientific laws, inescapable like gravitational pull, and valid regardless of historical context, unsusceptible to human ingenuity and progress. The second part of the double tragedy is that realist security is a zero-sum phenomenon, that is in increasing one's own security, the insecurity of others is also increased put simply, more soldiers, guns, may make a state feel more secure in the short term, but, in the longer term, those state made to feel secure by this build-up will conscript more soldiers and manufacture more military hardware in an effort to become more secure.

Neo realism and neorealist revision of security are fundamentally a response to perceived changes in the real world and unhappiness with realism's inflexibility in this context. Thus neo realism has also been significant in emphasizing structure at the expense of human nature in explaining the (lack of) agency of state actors. Neo realism in international relations did not arrive as an attack on the concept of security, rather its ideas and some of its theorists have had too broadly defined to be of any practical value or at least so contested vague that confusion is the inevitable result. Neo realism initially aimed to emphasize the importance of structural factors in explaining international dynamics rather than simply inherent evil human nature as classical and traditional realist strands had sought to do. Neo realism also sought to raise the profile the economic factors in the analysis of international relations. By highlighting the constraints of structure and the importance of economics, neo realism can clearly be seen as taking an important step towards greater relevance to the third world, although there are arguments to the country, since neo realism has based its structural approach on the sovereign state system, neo realisms role as a catalyst in moving to non-state based definitions is less contentious.

Comprehensive security by contrast, demonstrates two distinct shifts away from the states as the central unit of analysis, representing two opposite but ultimate interrelated foci. The first shift is towards focusing on the external community at large, as it has been shown that the rampaging forces of the environment and the ravaging effects of globalization go far beyond the ability of the state to contain them by its own resources. Epidemics like AIDS and other such diseases. Another such reminder is the series of financial crises hitting Europe (1990's) Latin America (1994-95) and Pacific Asia (1997-99).

The other trend is a shift inward from the states towards the individual citizen in term of human security. As defined by the United National Human Development Report of 1994, human security includes safety from chronic threats and harmful disruptions in the patterns of daily life. In the growing literature, the concept of human security has been expanded to include economic health and environmental concerns as well as physical security of the individual. After the 9/11 atmosphere of ubiquitous terror, which threatens the peace of mind and quality of life of the ordinary individual, is a new source of sinister threat to human security, in addition to being a threat to a country national security in the traditional sense.

Social Development:-

The world is passing through two fundamental revolutions that of rising expectations, and of information and communication, with both reinforcing each other. Awareness of the possibility and promise of better quality of life has percolated down to the remotest concerns of the world. But the actuality lags far behind. There is a gap between expectations and satisfaction. The impact is the greatest among youth where resorting to violence also comes early. This is reflected in the fact that the overwhelming majority of drug addicts and militants/ terrorist are in the age bracket of 15-30 years. The primary tools to deal with these challenges are political direction and an accelerated rate of socio-economic development. However, peace is the production for such development would be seriously jeopardize the nature of challenges to peace, therefore, acquire importance. The challenge of Narcotics Trafficking and transnational crime is another major problem, especially as it tends to acquire an ideological fig-leaf and natural external internal security dynamics is generated. Drug – Trafficking and it's interlink age with terrorism and militancy poses a serious threat to society and to state. Transnational support to narco-terrorism exacerbates the problem. In the external dimension, narcotics production and traffic has provided high levels of finance to fund proxy wars, insurgencies and transnational terrorism. India lies in the middle of two of the world's largest drug producing and exporting regions.

Threat of use and misuse of nuclear weapons have inevitably been carried out only when notable asymmetry existed between the threatening power and victim state. Compared to a single instance of the two nuclear bombs dropped in 1945. Almost invariably, such threats (and the use itself) took place when the victim state experienced adverse asymmetry. The factor of asymmetry, and the horrendous destructive potential of these weapons bestows on nuclear weapons. The power of immense political instrumentally. Nuclear disarmament, therefore, is not moral/ethical principle for us, based on a necessity for international peace and security, but an imperative for national security.

Economic Security (Geo-economics)

Recently, geo-economics has raised to rival, even out weight, geopolitics as a desideratum determining a country national interest and its foreign policy behavior. This has come about not only because of the end of the cold war but also more importantly, because of the globalization of the world economy beyond the stage of complex interdependence. The term 'geo-economics' has been much bandied about it needs a definition. On the macro level, in the geo-economics age, matters pertaining to manufacturing, marketing, financing and research and development are transnational and eventually, globalised. On the micro level, national power is no longer measured exclusively or even mainly, by a state if military might, and economic security has eclipsed through not displaced, military security on the scales of strategic importance to a country national interest.

The formulation which combines both macro- level economic power management and micro-level implications for individual states caught in a shifting power game, captures the essence of geo-economics as we use the term in this discourse, in addition to redefining power and what the new era power configuration imply, the formulation also points up the paramount of geo-economics calculations in the concerns of nations in world politics.

Environmental Security (Eco-politics)

Eco-politics, strictly speaking, has much broader connotation than the combination of the three terms economics, ecology and politics of which the term is contraction. In its original formulation by Dennis Pirages, "global eco-politics involves the use of environment issues, control over natural resources, scarcity arguments, and related concerns of social justice to overturn the international hierarchal expansion. As such eco-politics revolution encompasses a number of developments affecting all nations, subsumed under what pirages calls a new security," resulting from the exponential growth of population.

The threat of environmental degradation is far more serious than generally realized. Laster Brown has warned of the danger to humanity of climatic rise (global warming) due to increasing concentration of Co_2 (carbon dioxide) which had by 1998 hiked 31 percent in the two centuries since the industrial revolution. If Co_2 concentration doubles pre industrial levels during the twenty-first century as projected, global temperature is expected to rise by at least one degree, and as much as 4 degrees Celsius (or 2-7 degree Fahrenheit). Sea level is projected to rise from a minimum of 17 centimeters to as much as 1 meter by 2100.As Brown summarizes; this will alter every ecosystem on earth.

According to the latest reports, unusually high temperatures drought and forest fire brought suffering and death through the Europe continent and British Isles in the summer of 2003.preliminary estimates of farm losses alone rose to billions of dollors.the news proved that global warming is not a problem limited only to any particular or regional terrian.Considering the depleting fishery,forestry and other resources invoking the specter of global economic decline and raising doubts as to the sustainability of global economic development.Brown motto that we should be eplacing economics with ecology is a counsel of wisdom for all.Infact the earliest official recognition of environmental hazards as a threat to national security.

Human Security (Human Development)

Human security and human development falls into a continuum concerning human well being. The former deals with the psychological end state of development instead of the more mechanical aspects of human development. At a minimum, it is based on an individual and collective sense of protection from perceived present and potential threats to physical and psychological well being from all manner of agents and forces affecting lives, values, and property.

Human security is often subject to domestic structural conflict, or inequalities of society and brute atrocities by the victims own government as has happened with increasing frequency in the past two decades in Reanda and elsewhere, but these atrocities are not a monopoly of African nations. The Kosovo crisis dramatized the modern vulnerability of individuals to state aggression even in a European country.

Although the state terrorism is the most shocking and outrageous assault on the sanctity of human security other less dramatic, although no less disconcerting. Sources of human insecurity exist, such as .Income inequality, clean water shortage illiteracy, food shortage, housing shortage and infectious diseases.

Infectious diseases especially are a devastating for Africa. A reported 23 million people in sub Sahara Africa were said to have begun the twenty first century with a death sentence by HIV; the virus that leads to AIDS. For the first time in the modern era, life expectancy for an entire region is declining, threatening the economic future of 800 million people in sub-Sahara Africa; and it is declining by 20 years or more.

Poverty is one of the most threats to human security while an international conference on AIDS was being held in his country. Thabo Mbeki of South Africa was quoted by the New York Times, Fourth July 2000 as saying, "that extreme poverty rather than AIDS, was the tiger Killer" in South Africa president Mbeki was supported by no less prestigious an environmentalist than Bjorn Lombrog,

director of the environmental Assessment Institute in Denmark, who believed that the world should and global poverty before global warming.

References

1. John Baglas. *"International and global security in the post cold war era"*, in 2008.

2. William T. Ton & Russel Trood, *"Linkage Between traditional security and Human security"*, in ton, Thakur and Hyun, ed Asia Emerging Regional order, p.15

3. .Ramesh thakur, *"From National to Human Security"*, The Economic politics Nexus (Sidney: Allen & Unwin, 1998) p.53.

4. Cited in Gareth Porter, *Environmental Security as a National Security Issues"*, Current History May 1995 p.221.

5. Steven Walt *the Renaissance of security studies,* International studies Quarterly Vol.35 No.2pp. 211-239 1991.

6. Herz J *Idealists international and the security dilemma,* World Politics, 1950.

7. Buzan Barry & Lene Hense, *International Security,* London School of Economics & Political Science University of Correnphang 2007.

CHAPTER – II
ENERGY SECURITY BEING A STATE SECURITY

Energy Security and state security are closely interlinked. Energy Security plays an important role in the development of country. It enhances a nation's economic power and therefore, political status by providing it with the resources to pull its people out of poverty and pursue national growth and development. The European commission defines energy security as, "The ability to ensure that future essential energy needs can be met, both by means of adequate domestic resources worked under economically acceptable condition or maintained as strategic resources and by calling up an accessible and stable external sources supplemented appropriately by strategic stocks". For civilization energy has fundamental value. Energy security and even energy independency are critical to all countries energy security means sufficient depends on sustainable development of energy sphere. Currently energy resources such as coal and oil are becoming extremely depleted and will run out in the near future. The best replacement is the nuclear energy it is the fasts growing power generation industries in the world.

INTRODUCTION

The European commission defines energy security as, "The ability to ensure that future essential energy needs can be met, both by means of adequate domestic resources worked under economically acceptable condition or maintained as strategic resources, and by calling upon accessible and stable external sources supplemented where appropriate by strategic stocks". Bartan Redge Well Ronne, and Zilman defines it "As a condition which a nation and all most of its citizens businesses have access to sufficient energy resources at reasonable prices for the Foreseeable future free from serious risk of major disruption of service".

Although in the developed world the usual definition of energy security is simply the availability of inefficient supplies at affordable prices, different countries interpret what the concept means for them differently. Energy exporting countries focus and maintaining the security of demand for their export which after all generates the overwhelming share of their government revenues. Thus the usual definition varies from country to country. For Russia, the aim is to reassert state control over "strategic resources" and gain primary over the main pipelines market channels through its ships hydrocarbons to international markets. The concern for developing countries is about how changes in energy prices affect their balance of payments. For china and India, energy security lies in their ability to rapidly adjust to their new dependence on global markets, which represents a major shift away from their former commitments to self sufficiency. For Japan, it means offsetting its stark scarcity of domestic resources through diversification, trade and investment. In Europe, the major debate centers on how to manage dependence an imported natural gas and in most countries, a side from France and Finland, whether to build new power plants and perhaps to return to coal. And United States must face the uncomfortable fact that its goal of "energy independence" a phrase that has become a mantra since it was first articulated by Richard Nixen.

STATE SECURITY AND ITS CHANING NATURE

For civilization energy has fundamental value. Energy security and even energy independency are critical to all countries energy security means sufficient depends on sustainable development of energy sphere. Together energy production and energy consumption, distribution, transformation and exchange. The energy sphere covers the fuel energy complex power net works, power plants and energy consumers.

It is extremely difficult to ensure energy security and independence in the modern world. In the last 100 years world energy consumption has increased 12 times and has grown twice as fast as the earth population. Today one is focused with many serious problems. The energy sphere keeps growing at a pace that is incompatible with the health of the government, lead to an exhaustion of fossil-fuel resources. The growing demand energy can not be satisfied by further development of conventional energy technologies in the existing model of economy, based an fossil fuels, can not provide less developed countries, because the rates of growth of oil pumping in the world, is expected to slow down sharply. According to estimate, energy consumption will increase from the present 14 billion TCF (trillion cubic feet) up to 37 billion TCF by the end of the 21st century. Civilization faces a real threat to its existence coming not so much from political factors, but from contradictions between the level of economic development and the standards of material well being organized efforts for sustainable development and energy production and use are required from all national governments and the international organizations from all over world, as a whole. In many countries development programmes for energy industries, to cover next few decades, are being worked out. However, they do not take enough account of the global energy balance structure and the role of innovative technologies of the future.

Providing energy security is no longer a question of material resources; it involves a complicated structure consisting of laboratories national and international technologies initiatives, space exploration programmers, international networks, and education system, culture of energy consumption as well as traditional resources, plants and grids. On the eve of World War-1, first Lord of Admiralty Winston Churchill made a historical decision to shift the power source of the British navy ships from coal to oil. He intended to make the fleet faster than its German counterpart. But the switch also meant that the Royal Navy would rely not on coal form Wales but on insecure oil supplies from what was then Persia. Energy security thus became the question of national security. Churchill on "Safety and certainty in oil," lie in verity alone. Churchill's decision, energy security has repeatedly emerged as an issue of great importance, and it is so once again today. But the subject now needs to be rethought, for what has been the paradigm of energy security for the three decades is too limited and must be expanded to include many new factors. Moreover, it must be recognized that energy does not stand by itself but is lodged in the larger relations among nations and how they interact with one another.

The renewed focus on energy security is driven in part by an exceedingly tight oil market and by high oil prices, which have doubled over the past three years. It has also fuelled by the threat of terrorism, instability in some exporting nations, a nationalist backlash, and fear of a scramble of supplies, geopolitical rivalries, and countries fundamental need for energy to power their economic growth. The world will increasingly on new sources of supply from places where security systems are still being developed, such as the oil and natural gas fields offshore West Africa and in the Caspian Sea region, and the vulnerabilities are not limited to threats of terrorism, political turmoil, armed conflict and piracy. since Churchill's day, the key to energy security has diversification. This remain true, but a wider approach is now required that takes in to account the rapid evolution of the global trade, supply-chain vulnerabilities, terrorism and the integration of major new economies into the world market.

Internal Security of a state is considerable depends on the resource position. In other words, one can say that internal security cannot be maintained unless the national economy is sustained is not military hardware, through it may include it. Security is not military force, through it may encompass it security is development and without development there is no security. Threat to the development of a state, therefore, has to be viewed as a threat to internal security. It has been aptly said that in the changing scenario, the new world's battle ground are not territory, but market. Internal security of Asian nations in general and of India in particular would greatly depend up on development which can come about only through productive utilization of the abundant man power available, besides development of human resource and protection and expansion of market.

Threat to internal security is not perceived only within the geographical limit of defined territory of a state, but it extends beyond this would be evident from the fact that a state has to protect its territorial waters. There is no denying the fact that insurgency is a threat to internal security since the object of insurgency is to risk in an open rebellion against an established government and to usurp the control of Geo-Political system from the defacto government. Besides insurgency, terrorism violence, the regional movements adopting militant postures against the government or indulging in violent activites etc, are all serious threats to internal security.

REFERENCES

1. S.K. Chopra, Energy Policy for India: *"Towards sustainable energy security in India in twenty-first century"* Oxford & IBH publishing Co. Pvt. Ltd., New Delhi, and pp. 1342004.

2. Mikhail Y Pavlov, *"A New Energy Paradigm for the third Millennium"* world affairs, 2006 Vol 10, No. 1,pp.3.

3. Daniel yergin 2006, *"Ensuring Energy security".* Foreign affairs 2006 vol. 85 No.2, pp 69.

4. Michael Field, *A Hundred million dollars a day,* sidge wick & Jack Sew, landow 1975.

5. John Baglas. "International and global security in the post cold war era" ,in 2008

6. Morgenthau. H., Politics among nations: The struggle for power and peace, 5th edition Newyark Alford Knopt 1978

7. Michael Y Pavlov, "A New Energy Paradigm for the third Millennium" World Affaries,2006 vol 10,

8. Booth, k.and N.Wheeler; The Security Delima; Fear, Cooperation and Trust in World Politics. Basingstoke, Palgrave Macmillian.2008.

9. Corbet, P. Morals, Law and Power in international Relations. Los Angeles: J.R and D. Hayes Foundation. 1956.

10. Nye, J.S. The Power to lead: soft, Hard, and Smart, New York: Oxford University Press,

CHAPTER – III
ENERGY SCENARIO IN INDIA AND POLITICS

India is among the top four consumers of energy just behind the U.S, China, and Japan. India's total primary energy demand in 1997-98 was 25.5 million ton and this is expected to rise up to 770 million tons in 2020. Currently the sphere of fuels in primary energy dominated by coal and oil. India can not meet this demand domestically and has to rely on outside supplies. This creates a situation of dependence and call for cooperation from other nations-states. Currently energy resources such as coal and oil are becoming extremely depleted and will run out in the near future. The best replacement is the nuclear energy. It is the fastest growing power generation industries in the world, with this regard it is the safest, cleanest and most efficient. Today 15 percent of the world's electricity comes from nuclear power. As for the India's nuclear energy is concerned it is the fourth largest source of electricity. This industry is expected to under go a significant expansion in the coming years by passing the Indo-US nuclear deal, and than India is expected to generate an additional 25,000 MW of nuclear.

INTRODUCTION

Conventional sources of energy coal, petroleum and natural gas are the common sources. These account for about 90% of the demand for energy. Hydro- electricity and nuclear power accounts 10%. The elaborated figures are Oil 39.5%, Natural gas 19.6%, Coal 30.3%, Hydro power 6.7% and Nuclear 3.9%. The commercial energy consumption in the developed world has increased during last 3-4 decades. More than 80% of the total world consumption of energy is by 30% of the world population falling in the developing countries.

The energy scene in India is very complex. Important sources of non-commercial energy are fire wood, agriculture wastes and animal dung. Where as sources of commercial energy are coal lignite, oil, hydro electricity and to some extent atomic energy. Information on total energy for the period 1953-54 to 2000-2001 (CASE 1981) shows that proportion of non-commercial energy declined progressively from 67% in 1953-54 to 40% in 1980 commercial energy increased from 60.1 Million ton Coal replacement (MTCR) in 1953-54 to 249.3 MTCR in 1978-79 an average growth rage of 6%. The relative share of different forms of commercial energy in various sectors respectively oil constitutes 71.2% of house hold sector 61.8% agriculture and 83.9% of transport sector. While in industry it is coal (44.5%) and electricity (47.6%) that are important. According to Advisory Board on energy (ABE) that various forms of energy are likely to make the following contribution in India by 2004/2005, coal 450-540 mt, oil 90-110 mt, electricity 501-592 billion kwh, Non-commercial energy 500mt. The coal does not contribute significantly to house hold energy, though we have largely deposits of coal. According to ABE (1985) in rural sector 84% of lightening is by Kerosene and 94.5% cooking is a non-commercial fuel. In urban sector, lighting is 53% from electricity and 45.2% from kerosene were as cooking is 58.1% through non-commercial sources and 26.5% through kerosene.

The non- commercial sources of energy belong to two categories, 1. Renewable sources, like solar, wind, geothermal, microhydel etc and 2. Bio- mass based renewable system, like agricultural residues, biogas etc. The system in category second constitutes more than 50% of energy consumption for almost 80% of the energy consumption (ABE 1985). Increased application of fossil fuels (coal, petroleum and its products, natural gas) but also bio mass based (fire wood etc) systems in turn this help in conservation of resources as also in reducing environmental degradation. CASE 1981 summarized the state of knowledge on the application of new and renewable energy technologies and the present commercial fuel sources in different sectors. Similar analysis is done by Sootha (1984). It is evident that some devices like biogas, charcoal, fire wood, bio mass wind and solar energy have been developed and increasingly used in

India. In other energy system , there is scope for further improvement and also for cooperation with developed world.

India's policy for energy security

To meet the challenges of energy security, the vision 2025 document has set out an elaborate action plan for the acquisition of hydrocarbon resources required by the country to meet its economic requirements. It provides for a robust effort to expand domestic production of oil and gas through liberalization of the oil sector, encouragement to the entry of private Indian and foreign companies, investments in technology and R & D and so on. An important component of this effort is the external dimension which constitutes the area of India's "Oil diplomacy". This consists of substantial, robust and security interest. These overseas engagements are aimed at promoting the following;

a) Significant enhancement of domestic resources and capabilities by bringing in state of the art foreign technology by expending the national knowledge base.

b) Participation in downstream projects in producer and consumer countries on the basis of crisis-cross investments.

c) Finalization of long-term LNG contracts.

d) Setting up of transnational gas pipelines.

The contemporary international hydrocarbon environment is highly competitive, pitting corporations and nations against each other in ruthless contention and involving billions of dollars of financial flans and an occasion, even extra legal skullduggery. At the same time, this is also a period of unprecedented opportunity, with high oil prices opening up exploration and production prospects and compelling producer and consumer countries to pursue investments in the downstream sector, India's long term interests lie in putting together alliances and partnerships that would bring together different capabilities in joint proposals.

The petroleum ministry, over the last year, has engaged across the global carrying the massage of partnership and synergy in place of wasteful and unnecessary contention. Some of its significant interactions have been with the gulf countries, particularly Saudi-Arabia, Russia, the central Asian countries of Kazakhstan, Uzbekistan and Azerbaijan and Turkey and Romania that constitute the link between Central Asia and Europe. Other engagements have included Norway, Nigeria, some Latin American countries and most recently, China. The China diplomatic engagements have confirmed that the countries consumed are anxious to cooperate and that they see India a worth partner given its human capital and technical capabilities.

Saudi Arabia is India's largest supplies of crude oil meeting 25% of its annual requirements following the visit to India of King Abdul Aziz in January 2006. The two countries have agreed to transform their present commercial ties in to a

"Strategic Energy Partnership". This partnership is to be concretized through investment in each other down stream and petrochemicals projects as also through India's participation in Saudi Arabia's up stream proposals in the gas sector. Nothing that Saudi Arabia is the world's principal oil producer and India is a major hydrocarbon importer, the two countries. "Affirmed the important of stability in the oil market for the world economy". The Indian side proposed Saudi Arabia as a "trusted and reliable source of oil supplies to international market in general and the India market in particular".

India cooperation with Nigeria one of the world's principal oil producer is novel in that it is based on leveraging its hydrocarbon potential to promote domestic economic development project, the MOU concluded by the ONGC Mittal Joint Venture OMEL to set up a refinery power projects and railway lines and equipment in exchange for two oil blocks on nomination basis, a long term contract for supply of oil, and access to gas once the LNG facilities have been set up. This pioneering approach to bilateral cooperation, could serve as a model for India's interaction with other African countries which have a rich hydrocarbon potential even as they need considerable inputs of capitals for their economic and infrastructure development. Four countries i.e. Russia, Japan Norway and Republic of Korea have emerged as important partners for India companies for the development of domestic resources and capabilities, covering issues such as, increased oil recovery (IOR) and enhanced oil recovery (EOR) commercial and strategic storage, promotion of conservation and of environmental friendly fuels, training , health and safety development of unconventional energy resources such as coal bed methane, underground coal gasification and gas hydrates, and above all, pursuing equality participation and E & P proposals in third countries.

Indian oil diplomacy has already begun to yield concrete results. India has a 25% equity participation in an oil producing field in Sudan, which provides India with three million tons /Annum. Other producing fields in which India has equity states are in Russia, Vietnam and Myanmar; India has also secured E and P contracts in Iran, Egypt, Quarter, Nigeria, Libya, Syria and Cuba.

Coal is the domestic commercial fuel in India .Satisfying more than half of India's energy demand. Domestic supply satisfies most of India's coal requirements owing to the fact, that India is the world's third largest coal producer (after China and U. S) power generation account for about 70% of India's coal is consumption, followed by heavy industry. Indian coal is generally highly in ash content and is low calorific value and so most of the cooking coal is imported. Coal consumption is projected in the international energy annual 2004 to increase to 430 million short tons in 2010 up from 359 million short tons in 2000. Major Indian coal fields are found in Bihar, West

Bengal, and M.P. There has been effort to privatize the coal industry in the past, but the current government has called off plans for further coal-sector liberalization in the face of strong opposition from labor unions.

Recognizing the need of alternatives for fossil fuel, a committee a Development of Bio-fuel was constituted with exports from planning commission in July 2002 in its report in July 2003, it proposed bio-ethanol and bio-diesel as respectively and ministry of rural development (MORD) was made the Nodal Ministry for implementation of its recommendation by the PMO.

Ministry of petroleum and natural Gas (MOP & NG) mandated 5% ethanol blending from January 2003 in nine states. (Maharashtra, Gujarat, Goa, Haryana, U.P, Punjab, Karnataka, Andhra Pradesh & Tamil Nadu) and four union territories (Daman-Div, Dadra & Nagar Haveli, Pondicherry and Chandigarh) using molasses as feed stock. However, production of sugarcane and molasses in 2003-2004 fell short due primarily of draught, the 5% ethanol blending target could not be met and hence it was subsequently, revived in November 2006. In October 2007 GOL extended the norm of mandatory 5% blending of ethanol across the country and set a target of 10% blending of ethanol from October 2008. Prices of ethanol was fixed at Rs. 21.5 per liter for the next three years and further production of ethanol directly from sugarcane Juice apart from molasses was also approved.

Diesel is used for 80% of our country's transport and rest is petrol. Hence, apart from ethanol blended petrol, bio diesel from non edible oil seed crop such as Jatropua and Pongamia is viewed as another viable option. In order to promote the nascent bio diesel industry the GOL initiated national mission on bio-diesel with MORD as the nodel agency and set targets for blending with high speed Diesel at 5% in 2006-2007 to be increased to 20% in 2011-2012. This would require 13.38 MMT of bio diesel (20% of 66.9 MMT of HSD) to obtained from 11.2 million Ha. Of Jatropha plantation). In an effort to promote India's emerging bio-diesel policy has been approved by the group of ministers

(GOM) headed by union minister for Agriculture shared Power in its second meeting on 19 july 2008, to be sent for cabinet's approval. The policy is claimed to offer a balanced approach to fulfill the country's growing energy and food security needs particularly at a time when the food prices are rising alarmingly due to the partly to the conversion of cultivable land from food to fuel crops. By incentivizing cultivation of alternative bio fuel such as Jatropha through subsides for the growers and a minimum support prices mechanism at the production and of the China, the policy also proposes subsides and fiscal concession further upstream for collection and marketing of oil, seeds, a five year financial support package for bio fuel processing industries and to cover R & D, quality management and testing and to certification for mandatory blending requirements for automobiles. A national mission on bio diesel with a budget of rupees 1340 corer for five years and the phase first of the mission the demonstration of commercial Jatropha cultivation over 400000 Ha. Were also proposed by the ministry of rural development. A nation bio fuel coordination committee chaired by the Prime Minister Manmoham Singh would be formed to deal with all the issues relevant to be bio fuels until national bio fuel development board comes into existence.

Domestic heating and water supply can be met by solar energy. In Israel, such system of heating homes and water supply is already in operation. In USA commercial solar heaters are available in Florida and California. In Asia, Africa and Australia where number of sunshiny days are high, this method has promising future. These receive abundant sunshine with about 1648-2108 KWH/m2 // year with nearly 250-300 days of useful sunshine in a year. The daily solar energy incidence is between 5 to 7 Kwh/m2 at different parts of the country. This enormous solar energy resource may be conversion routes. The solar thermal routes uses radiation in the form of heat that in turn may be converted to mechanical, electrical or chemical energy. Solar thermal devices, like solar cookers, solar water/air heaters, solar dryers, solar wood seasoning kilns and Silicon system have been developed.

According to the minister of new and renewable energy (MNRE), grid interactive solar power at the end of March

2007, stood at 2.93 MW in the country. The ministry had set a target of generating 50 MW during the 11ᵗʰ plan period. Solar energy efforts were further boosted when the government announced the long awaited 'semi conductor policy' which proposes incentives for semi conductor use and manufacturing that include tax exemptions and subsides.

Besides investing $40 million to set up a module manufacturing unit producing 50 MW, Solar semi conductor which has office in Hyderabad and Sunyvale, U S has begged an order worth E10 million (55 corer) from a European company for a supply of high quality solar Photo Voltaic (PV) modules, Kolkata based Environ Energy tech service announced the acquisition of Netherland's based shell's solar energy business in India, & Srilanka with this, the company aims to become the largest photovoltaic panel based solar solution company worldwide and expects to achieve a turnover or rupees 150 corer by March 2008. Sharp business systems also recently announced the launch of its solar business in India and aims to capture over 20% of the 600 corer domestic market by 2010.

As for the India's nuclear energy is concerned it is the fourth-largest source of electricity, after the thermal hydro and renewable sources of electricity. As for 2008, India has 17 Nuclear Power Plants in operation generating 4, 1200 MW while 6 other are under construction and are expected to generate an additional 3,160 MW. India being a non signatory of the Nuclear Non-proliferation treaty (NPT) has been subjected to a defected nuclear embargo from members of the nuclear suppliers Group (NSG) cartel. India is expected to generate an additional 25000 MW of nuclear power by 2020, bringing total estimate nuclear power generation to 45000 MW.

REFERENCES

1. Ahmad Talmid, *"oil diplomacy for India's energy security challenges and opportunities"* Foreign service Institute New Delhi 2007.

2. Bio fuels in India: *An Assessment of key Socio-Economic and Environmental issues* a project proposal, Kasturi Das Centered 4th April 2008.

3. What's right with bio-fuel (w.w.w.iaa.org/journalist/arch)

4. NSG clears nuclear waiver for India (w.w.w /bniline.com/new/nsg 2008.

5. India Joins Nuclear club gets NSG waiver (www.ndtv.com).

6. Shahi R. V., India's Strategy towards energy development and energy security, Secretary to the Govt. of India.

7. Tongia, Rahul., "Whither Nuclear Power" Economic and political weekly March 25 2006.

8. Norris, R. and H. Kristensen, Global nuclear inventories, 1945- 2010, Bulletin of the Atomic Scientists. 2010.

9. Smith, M.E, International Security: Politics, Policy, Prospects. Basingstoke: Palgrave Macmillan.2010.

10. Donney, J. Realism and international Relations. Cambridge: Cambridge University Press. 2000.

CHAPTER –IV
NUCLEAR ENERGY AND NUCLEAR PROLIFERATION

Currently energy resources such as coal and oil are becoming extremely depleted and will run out in the near future. The best replacement is the nuclear energy. It is the fastest growing power generation industries in the world, with this regard it is the safest, cleanest and most efficient, today 15 percent of the world's electricity comes from nuclear power. There are different technologies that are used in reactors often dependent on the fuel used to power. The most common is uranium including uranium 235 used in light water reactors, and uranium 238 uses in faster breeder reactors. There has always been acute awareness of the fact that some of the materials technologies and expertise that are relevant for peaceful use of nuclear energy can be used equally for making nuclear weapons. India conduct a nuclear test in 1974 partly in response of external challenges, however, it claimed that the detonation was a peaceful explosion. India also did not sign on NPT & CTBT also due to its external challenges from various countries. Through this reason India facieses number of sanctions many of which were lifted by late 2000AD.

INTRODUCTION

Currently energy resources such as coal and oil and becoming extremely exploited and will run out in the near future. Nuclear energy has the potential of becoming the most effective type of energy. The world has ever seen. Electricity from nuclear fission continues to be the most comprehensive source of energy available to meet the growing demand of the world, with regards to all major energy sources. Nuclear energy is by for the safest, cleanest, and most efficient one ton of uranium produces more energy than is produced by several million tons of coal and several million barrels of oil.

There are different technologies that are used in reactors often dependent on the fuel used to power. The most common is uranium including uranium 235 used in light water reactors, and uranium 238 uses in faster breeder reactors. U-238 comprises over 99% of the total natural uranium reserves. Thorium which more commonly found than uranium is an alternative where U-233 obtained from the thorium fuel cycle.

NUCLEAR ENERGY

Today more than 15 percent of the world's electricity comes from nuclear power. The united states have 110 commercial reactors about one fifty of the nation's electricity, this shows that U.S.A. has more reactors than any country in the world. France and Japan are two countries that have also large dependence on nuclear power. Nuclear based capacity in France is 63.2 GW (57 percent total installed capacity) while that Japan 45.9 GW (19 percent of the total installed capacity. The share of nuclear in France went up from 25.3% in 1980 to 78% in 2003 In Japan the share of nuclear power increased from 14.3% in 1980 to 23%.

As for the India's nuclear energy is concerned it is the fourth largest source of electricity. After thermal, hydro and renewable sources of generating. As for 2008, India has 17 nuclear power plants in operation to generate an additional 3,160 MW. The Indian nuclear power industry is expected to undergo a significant expansion in the coming years through the passing of the Indo-Us nuclear deal. This agreement will allow India to carry out trade of nuclear fuel and technologies with other countries and significantly enhance its power generations capacity. India is expected to generate an additional 25000 MW of nuclear power by 2020, bringing total estimate nuclear power generation to 45000MW. India's nuclear power plants, currently, seventeen nuclear power reactors produce 4120 MW (2.9% of total installed base).

The nuclear industry continues to provide electricity competitive rates and several countries in need of additional generation capacity are going ahead with plans to set up nuclear plants, a divergent view is also expressed that nuclear is not cost competitive. In early 2005, the nuclear energy agency and international energy agency released their joint report titled, "Projected Costs of Generating Electricity", 2005 update with the objective to provide reliable information on key factors affecting the economics of electricity generation using a range of technology (NEA 2005).The report gives cost ratio's of electricity generations from nuclear and coal, and also from nuclear and gas. At 5% discount rate, nuclear is cheaper as compared to gas in the 19 countries. At 10% discount, rate, except Japan and the USA nuclear is cheaper compared to gas. At 5% discount rate except South Korea and the USA, nuclear is cheaper as compared to coal. At 10% discount rate, in South Korea, USA and Germany, nuclear is cheaper compared to coal.

Nuclear Power and Carbon Emission:-

In 2003, India's carbon dioxide emission from fossil fuels combustion stood at 1024 million tons, out of which 666 million tons were from coal. India is the world's fifth 5th largest Co2 emitter after USA, China Russia and Japan (Energy Information Administration 2005). Further, India's Co2 Emission grew faster than these countries an annual growth rate of 5.5 % (1980-2003) as against 4% of China, 1% of USA and 1% of Japan. By 2025, China is projected to be the world's largest Co2 emitter followed by USA and India (Energy Information Administration 2005). Large scale deployment of nuclear power could partly be a solution to the Co2 problem. India adding about 20000 MW by 2015 and 32000 MW by

2020. Consequently India will reduce its reliance on coal to that extent.

Table: Estimate of present and future power sector coal demand CO2 emission.

Year	Scenario	Coal Consumption in power station	CO2 emission from coal in power sector
2005	Present	265 mt	477 mt
2015	No significant nuclear	520-630 mt	930-1160 mt
2015	20 GW of nuclear capacity	420-500 mt	780-1000 mt
2020	No significant nuclear	640-770 mt	1160-1380 mt
2020	32 GW of nuclear capacity	500-640 mt	910-1140 mt

CO2 emission for this scenario with the addition of 20 GW of nuclear capacity, the coal required can be reduced by at least 150 million tons per annum. If this trend of building nuclear power station continues them by 2020 India would reduce about CO2 emission by at least 250 million tons per annum. This amount is not small considering that the present annual CO2 emission from and United Kingdom   (U K) are 409 and 564 million tons respectively (EIA 2005).

France and Japan are two countries that have a large dependence as nuclear power. Nuclear based capacity in France 57% total installed capacity while the Japan 19% of the total installed capacity. The share of nuclear in France and Japan went up in 2003 on words. Thermal Power still dominates at 63%. As a result, the carbon emission in France has declined over the past two decades. While the Japan the emissions have marginally up reflecting its greater reliance on thermal power.

Share of thermal and nuclear generation in France, India and Japan, 1980 and 2003.

Country	Thermal generation		Nuclear generation	
	1980	2003	1980	2003
France	47.0	10.3	25.3	78.0
India	58.0	84.3	2.5	2.9
Japan	69.0	63.7	14.3	23.3

Nuclear Proliferation

There has always been an acute awareness of the fact that same of the materials, technologies and expertise's that are relevant for the peaceful use of nuclear energy can also be equally of use for making nuclear weapons. Since the launching of "Atom for peace" programme in 1953, the promotion of the peaceful uses of nuclear energy has therefore, invariably been linked to policies and measures for preventing the proliferation of nuclear weapons. By and large, this two pronged approach has been successfully. There are now same 450 nuclear power plants and an even large number of facilities for other applications of nuclear energy (e.g. in medicine agriculture and industry).

On 16th July 1945, the United States detuned the world's first nuclear explosive device at Alamogordo, New Mexico. The detonation, small by current standards was equivalent of 21000 tons of higher explosives. The atomic bomb caused grave concern about the future of U.S national security most understood that the United States could not base its security indefinitely in its monopoly of atomic weapons.

Now eight (08) countries are known to possess nuclear weapons in order to their acquisition of nuclear arms. They are the United States (1945). The Soviet Union (1948), the united kingdom (1952), France (1960) China (1964) Israel (1967) India (1974) and Pakistan (1989). The other states are thought to be actively pursuing nuclear weapons, most notably Iran, North Korea and Libya. (Now Iran is going to nuclear deal with America). Given the central role of these weapons in international affairs. South Africa acquired nuclear weapons in 1979 but eliminated its nuclear arsenal in 1991.

Nuclear Weapon States since 1945.

1995--10----------North Korea
1990--08---------South Africa

1985--	09--------	Pakistan
1980--	08----------	South Africa
1975--	07----------	India
1970--	06----------	Israel
1965--	05----------	China
1960--	04---------	France
1955--	03----------	United Kingdom
1950--	02----------	Soviet Union
1945--	01----------	United States

In terms of scale, the United States and Russia each deploy roughly 6000 (six thousand) war heads a strategic (long-range) system and retain. According to one unclassified estimate, several thousand tactical nuclear weapons (deployed on shorter range delivery systems are available for rapid deployment on them). The other three longs recognized nuclear power Great Britain, France and China. The Israeli, Indian and Pakistani capabilities are considerably smaller. North Korean capabilities are minute. Even of US and Russian arsenals were reduced to 1700-2200 deployed strategic warheads as agreed by Russia & the united states in the May 2002 Moscow treaty. The overall destruction power of those forces would continue to eclipse that of the other nuclear states for the foreseeable future.

In the five nuclear weapon states announced their arrival as members of the nuclear club unambiguously, either with the combat use of deploy nuclear weapons or atmospheric nuclear test, with left no doubt their capabilities. The situation was for more complexes for the other nuclear weapon states, however, by the time these states achieved the ability to deploy nuclear weapons, U.S. and international concerns about nuclear proliferation had intensified to the point that it was advantageous for those states to avoid out right acknowledgement of their nuclear weapons status. India conducts a nuclear test in 1974 partly in response to external challenges, partly for domestic political reasons. It claimed, however, that the detonation was a peaceful explosion of the type the U.S and soviet Union were than exploring to excavate harbors and to fracture geologic strata to facilitate oil and nature gas production. India did not declare itself to be a nuclear power until it conducted a seemed series of nuclear tests in may 1998. The latter tests were apparently motivated by its desire to develop warheads for a missile based deterrent against China before mounting pressures for India to join the Comprehensive Test Ban Treaty (CTBT) made testing political infeasible.

Pakistan, perceiving itself under continuing threat from the larger and more powerful India, apparently assembled its first nuclear weapon in 1989. Pakistan did not declare itself weapons state until 1998. When it conducted a series of nuclear tests to match India's.North Korea's nuclear status is uncertain.It denies it has used its nuclear facilities to produce nuclear weapons.The U.S Government, however, has stated that Korea possesses sufficient nuclear weapon material (Plutonium) for one to two nuclear devices, presumably acquired to intimidate U.S. backed South Korea and to compensate for its loss of Soviet support after the end of Cold War. If, over the course of the 1990s North Korea formed this Plutonium in to nuclear weapons. Than North Korea needs to be counted as a member in to nuclear club.

The treaty on the Non- Proliferation of nuclear weapons, also Nuclear Non-Proliferation Treaty (NPT or NNPT) is a treaty to limit the spread of nuclear weapons, opened for signature as July 1, 1968; there are currently 189 countries party to the treaty, five of which have nuclear weapons. The United States of America, the United Kingdom, France , Russia, and the People's Republic of China (the five permanent members of the united Nation Security Council). Only the four recognized sovereign states are not parties to the treaty. India, Israel, North Korea, and Pakistan have openly tested and possess nuclear weapons. Israel has had a policy of opacity regarding its own nuclear weapons program. North Korea acceded to the treaty, violated it and later withdrew. The treaty was proposed by Ireland, and Finland, was the first to sign. The signing parties decided by consensus to extend the treaty indefinitely and without conditions up on meeting in New York City on May 11, 1995. The nuclear non proliferation treaty consists on a preamble and eleven articles.

REFERENCES

1. NSG clear nuclear waiver for India (w.w.w ibnlive.caw/new/nsg2008.

2. India Joins Nuclear club gets NSG waiver (w.w.w.ndtv.com)

3. Official website of the international atomic energy agency (IAEA) http,/wwwiaea.org

4. Robert, F.Goheen., "Indo-Us relations: Nuclear Proliferation and technology transfer". New Delhi 1984 pp.153-55

5. H.W. Brands., India and the United States: The cold peace. Bosten 1990

6. Kapur, Ashok.,India's Nuclear option: Atomic diplomacy decision making New York 1979.

7. Prasad, Basudo, Yadav, Indo-Us Civil Nuclear Cooperation Agreement P.D. October 2008.

8. Spector, Leonard. S, Nuclear Proliferation; The spread of nuclear weapons New York, 1984.

9. Kapur, K.D., Nuclear Non Proliferation Diplomacy ; Nuclear Power Program in the third world. New Delhi London publisher 1993.

10. Bharadwaj, Anshu, India's future electric power requirements and role of nuclear energy, Econmic and Political weekly , march 25 , 2006.

CHAPTER –V
INDO- US NUCLEAR DEAL AND ENERGY SECURITY

In recent times security is being interpreted increasingly as comprehensive security, the focus has been shifted towards the human security, economic security and as well as the environmental security. Energy security and state security plays an important role in the development of country. It enhances a nation's economic power and therefore, political status by providing it with the resources to pull its people out of poverty and pursue national growth and development. The Indo-US nuclear agreement all show case the increasing importance of energy as a driver of national and international politics. The ambit of the deal includes research, development, design construction, operation, maintenance and use of nuclear reactors, reactor experiments and decommissioning. The US will have the right to seek return of nuclear fuel and technology but it will compensate for the costs incurred as a consequence of such removal. India can develop a strategic reserve of nuclear fuel to guard against any disruption of supply over the life time of its reactors.

INTRODUCTION

Currently energy resources such as coal and oil are becoming extremely depleted and will run out in the near future. The best replacement is the nuclear energy. Nuclear energy refers to the use of any nuclear technology to extract usable energy from atomic nuclei via controlled nuclear reaction. Now it is the fastest growing power generation Industry in the world, with this regard nuclear energy is the safest, cleanest and most efficient. One ton of uranium produces more energy, than is produced by several million tons of coal or several million barrels of oil. The most common is uranium 235 used in light water reactors, and uranium 238 comprises over 99% of the total natural uranium reserves. Thorium which more commonly found than uranium is an alternative where U-235 obtained from the thorium fuel cycle.

Today more than 15 percent of the world's electricity comes from nuclear power. The united states of America (USA) have 10 commercial reactors that generating about one fifth of the nations electricity. As for the India's nuclear energy is concerned it is the fourth (4th) largest source of electricity. After thermal, hydro and renewable sources of electricity. As for 2008, India has 17 nuclear power plants in operation generating 4,120 MW while 6 other are under construction and are expected to generate an additional 3160MW.

India's emergence in the world nuclear scene was not a new phenomenon. In fact it had been Jawaharlal Nehru's aim to use atomic energy for peaceful purposes it was his initiative that had led to the establishment of the India atomic energy commission in August 1948. The non proliferation treaty of 1968 was not signed by India, as India thought that it would be a major hurdle of peaceful experiments.

NUCLEAR ENERGY

The importance of nuclear energy is an alternative to oil based power. This statement comes at a time when spiraling oil prices and growing concern over climate change have led to governments around the world expression a renewed interest in nuclear energy. Nuclear energy is, in the medium term, the nearest thing to a non-polluting energy source capable of generating power on a large scale we have solar energy is an option, but only on the long term a lot of research and development is required before it can be capable of handling the energy needs of a nation on a sustained basis.

The biggest advantage of nuclear energy is, of course, its non-reliance on oil. Its lack of carbon emission is a well become side benefit. And third generation nuclear reactors minimize the risk of leakage, as the Japanese experience has proven. Give the global electricity consumption is expected to double in the next few decades while oil prices go through the roof, the attitude towards nuclear energy was bound to change. Technological advances are making its use safer more economical.

The 2006 expert committee on energy estimated India's power needs at 990, 00 MW by 2031-32, up from 114000 MW today. This assumed a GDP growth rate of 9% which is very optimistic. But if indeed India grows so fast, coal, hydel and non-conventional energy sources will meet at best 75% of India's needs in 2030, and this proportion will keep declining as coal reserves deplete, then only nuclear energy alone can fill this gap. The gap and India's need for nuclear energy will keep rising in future decades.

India's relations with the United States of America since independence have been a major factor in India's foreign policy calculation. India's relation with the U.S. has never remained constant in the last sixty years. It has often varied between normal and sometimes bitter relationships. The relationship has been marked by instability and fluctuations, within limited instability; there has been either violent conflict or virtual alliance in the wavering course of this relationship. At no point of time have the relations broken down completely, while the national interest has been something basic to the structure and functioning of the foreign policy of both the countries. They have been clashing over a number of issues whether international as well as regional significance.

Historically, India was inspired by the American declaration of independence, and aspired for the American ideas of progress and democracy. The United States supported India's freedom movement as was evident in 1941 when the U.S. state department had advised Britain to grant temporary dominion status to India, so that India' whole hearted supported could be gained to carry on the war effectively. Subsequently, India's policy towards the United States of America was indicated in the first policy statement of Jawaharlal Nehru on September 7, 1946. Nehru acknowledged the dominant role that the United States of America was destined to play in the world affairs and stated. We send our greetings to the people of United States of America to whom destiny has given a major role in international affairs. We trust that this tremendous responsibility will be utilized for furtherance of peace and human freedom everywhere.

Difference over nuclear issues greatly complicated the overall course of Indo-U.S relationship since the late 1960's. During 1970's this issue becomes much, more complicated. The two countries came to a sort of clash on the U.S. reluctance to supply fuel to India for Tarapur Atomic Power Station (TAPS). It was a reflection of their ideological stands on the NPT taken at the global level. The U.S. nuclear non-proliferation act of 1978 made the supply of nuclear fuels to any non-nuclear (power) weapons country conditional on its acceptance of international in its objective of limiting nuclear arms pressurized the non-nuclear power to adhere to non-proliferation treaty. The U.S. Congress pressed even harder, called for cut off of economic aid to countries not accepting international safeguards against the spread of nuclear weapons, including intrusive inspection. In the 1980's India tried to improve its relations with the United States which had reached to a very low level particular over the nuclear issues which had become a major bone of contention between the two countries. Indian efforts towards this direction were necessary for gaining recognition of its primary in the region by both super powers. It was help to India in reaching an amicable solution to Tarapur issue. It was in pursuit of these objectives that Indra Gandhi met president Reagan in Cancun in 1981.she made an official visit to the united States in 1982 which successfully resolved the important issue of the TAPS nuclear fuel supply. France agreed to supply fuel with the United States consent. Speaking about India's nuclear policy in Lok-Shaba, Indra Gandhi informed the house on February 24, 1983 that the policy of government of India was to utilize atomic energy for peaceful purposes and continued to be the same.

Thus, during the years 1947-1948, Indo-US relations experienced ups and downs frequently. In the post second world war era, the basic objectives of American foreign policy were to contain communism and Soviet Union's expansionism. But India followed a positive and dynamic policy of non-alignment. It did not align with either power bloc and firmly followed the policy of non-alignment did not get enmeshed in to the cold war politics of military alliances. India came into direct confrontation with the US on various international forms on v various important issues which run counter to the United States of America's policies and interests, which largely remained responsibly for serve strains in the relations between the two countries.

India's continued efforts to improve relations with U.S. under Rajiv Gandhi's tenure in effect witnessed crystallization of the "opening" made in aftermath of Indira Gandhi's visit to U.S. in 1982. This resulted in a more multifaceted relationship between the two countries, involving security, economic, scientific and technological, and defense cooperation. His visit to the U.S. during 11-15th June 1985 was in same way a landmark in Indo-U.S political strategic relations. The signing and finalization of the memorandum of understanding between the two countries become the basis for the export of U.S. advanced "duel" technology of India and opened new avenues for Indo-U.S cooperation.

Civil Nuclear Agreement:

The Indo- Us civilian nuclear agreement, known also as the Indo-US nuclear deal, refers to a bilateral accord on civil nuclear cooperation between the United States of America and the republic of India. The frame work for this agreement was a July 18, 2005 joint statement by Indian Prime Minister Dr. Manmohan Singh and U.S. President George W. Bush, under which India agreed to separate its civil and military nuclear facilities and place all its civil nuclear facilities under

International Atomic Energy Agency (IAEA) safeguards and, in exchange, the United States agreed to work towards full civil nuclear cooperation with India. The US-India deal took more than three years to come to fruition as it had to go through several complex stages, including the amendment of US domestic law, a civil military nuclear separation plan in India, an India IAEA safeguards (inspections) agreement and the grant of an exemption for India by the Nuclear Suppliers Group (NSG0, and export control cartel that had been formed mainly in response to India's first nuclear test in 1974. It its final shape, the deal under permit safeguards those nuclear facilities that India has identified as "civil" and permits broad civil nuclear cooperation, while excluding the transfer of "sensitive" equipment and technologies including civil enrichment and reprocessing items even under IAEA safeguards. On August 18, 2008 the IAEA board of Governors approved, and on February 2, 2009 India signed on India-specific safeguards agreement with IAEA.

The nuclear deal was widely seen as a legacy building effort by President Bush and Prime Minister Singh. But while the deal had to pass with the US congress twice (one when Hydel act was passed in late 2006 to amend US domestic law and then when the final real-related package was approved in October 2008) Singh blocked the Indian Parliament from scrutinizing the deal. The deal proved very contentious in India and threatened at one time to topple Singh's government which survived a confidence vote in parliament in July 2008 by stopping in a regional party as a coalition partner in place of the leftist block that had bolted.

In August 1, 2008, the IAEA approved the safeguards agreement with India, after which the United States approached the Nuclear Suppliers Group (NSG) to grant a waiver to India to commence civilian nuclear trade. The 45 nation NSG granted the waiver to India on September 6, 2008 allowing it to access civilian nuclear technology and fuel from other countries. The implementation of this waiver make India the only known country with nuclear weapons which is not a party to the non-proliferation treaty (NPT) but is still allowed to carry out nuclear commerce with the rest of the world. The US House of Representatives passed a bill on 28 September 2008. Two days later, India and France linked a similar nuclear pact taking France the first country to have such an agreement with India. On October 1, 2008 the US senate also approved the civilian nuclear agreement allowing India to purchase nuclear fuel and technology from United States. United States president George W Bush Signed the legislation on the Indo- US nuclear deal , approved by the congress, into law, now called the United States, India Nuclear Cooperation Approval and non=proliferation enhancement Act, on October 8, 2008.

The proposal civil nuclear agreement implicitly recognizes India's   "defacto" status even without signing the NPT. The

Bush administration satisfies a nuclear pact with India because it is important in helping to advance the non-proliferation framework by formally recognizing India's strong non-proliferation record even though it has not signed the NPT. The former undersecretary of state of political affairs, Nicholas Burns, one of the architects of the Indo-US nuclear deal said, India's trust, its credibility, the fact that it has promised to create a art facility, monitored by the IAEA, to begin a new export control regime in place, because it has not proliferated the nuclear technology we can't say about Pakistan. However, members of the IAEA safeguards staff have made it clear that Indian demands that New Delhi be allowed to determine when Indian reactors might be inspected could undermine the IAEA safeguards system. The reason for this is to restrict development of nuclear weapons and to negotiate with India indirectly to ratify the NPT using another mechanism.

Financially, the United States also expects that such a deal could spur India's economic growth and bring in and 150$ million in the next decade for nuclear power plants, of which the United States wants a share. It is India's stated objective to increase the production of nuclear power generation from its present capacity of 4000 mwe to 20000 mwe in the next decade. However, the developmental economic advising from Dalberg, which advises the IMF and the World Bank, moreover, has done its own analysis of the economic valve of investing in nuclear power development to India. Their conclusion is that for the next 20 years such investments are likely to be far less valuable economically or environmentally than the variety of other measures to increase electricity production in India. They have noted that United States nuclear vendors cannot sell any reactors to India unless and until India caps third party liabilities or establishes a credible liability pool to protect U.S. firms from being sued in the case of an accident or a terrorist act of sabotage against nuclear plants.

India powered its way on 6 September 2008 into global nuclear fold after the Nuclear Suppliers Group (NSG) rewrote its guidelines for resuming nuclear trade with New Delhi. The decision to admit India came after three days of intense diplomacy by the U.S.in the nuclear cartel that controls the global flow of nuclear fuel and technologies. The Nuclear Suppliers Group (NSG) acceptance of the U.S. proposal to drop the ban on nuclear trade will now go to the U.S. congress for up-down approval before it adjourns in end –September for elections.

Having failed to use its proxies effectively, China had come out in the open with its opposition to the deal. In a bid to prevent China hijacking the proceeding, U.S. President Bush wrote a letter to Chinese President, Huo Jintao asking Beijing to support the India waiver. But the real opposition come from the non proliferation ideologies. The Netherlands, Norway,

Switzerland, Ireland, Austria, and New Zeeland, who were persuaded one by until Austria remained the last country standing against the waiver. The last minute changes to the draft combined with the softening of position of others finally wore down Austria's resistance. Than the 45 nations NSG granted the waiver to India allowing it to access civilian nuclear technology and fuel from other countries. France was the first country to have such an agreement with India.

REFERENCES

1. Robert, F. Goheen., *"Indo-Us relations: Nuclear Proliferation and technology".* New Delhi 1984.

2. House of reps clears N-deal, France set to sign agreement us world "the times of India" 2008 Oct.

3. *"India's Nuclear- Diplomacy"* Kaushalendra Mishra, Navyug publishers and Distributors New Delhi, 2009.

4. The Economist *"The end of cheap food"* Economic times June 2008.

5. Shahi R.V., *"India's strategy towards energy development and energy security;* secretary to the Govt. of India"

6. .H.W.Brands.,India and the United States: The cold peace Bosten 1990,p.162

7. S.P.Limaya, US-Indian relations: The pursuit of accommodation Boulder:Calarado,1993.

8. Mohite,Dilip, H., Indo –Us Relations: Issues in conflict and cooperation New Delhi south Asian publisher, 1995.

9. Ouapally, Deepa, Nuclear cooperation: challenges and cooperation Banglore: National institute of Advanced studies, 1997.

10. Rana, A.P, ed, Four Decades of indo-us Relations: A commemorative retrospective, New Delhi Haranand publication, 1994.

11. Sultan, Adil Mohammad., Indo-Us Civilian Nuclear cooperation Agreement; Implication on south Asian Security Environment. Stimson Center July 2006.

CHAPTER –VI
INDO-US NUCLEAR DEAL AN ASSESSMENT

Energy security and the state security are closely interlinked. Energy security plays an important role in the development of country. It enhances a nation's economic power and therefore, political status by providing it with the resources to pull its people out of poverty and pursue national growth and development. The purpose of the (Indo-US Nuclear deal) agreement is to enable full civil nuclear and energy cooperation between the India and the United States. The agreement provides full civil nuclear energy cooperation covering nuclear reactors and aspects of the associated nuclear fuel cycle including enrichment and reprocessing. This agreement also opens the door for cooperation in civil nuclear energy with other countries. The ambit of the deal includes research, development, design, construction operation maintenance and use of nuclear reactors, rector experiments and decommissioning. This agreement has 17 articles which deal with definitions, scope of protection, transfer of nuclear material and related technology.

INTRODUCTION

The importance of nuclear energy is an alternative to oil based power. This statement comes at a time when spiraling oil prices and growing concern over climate change have led to governments around the world expression a renewed interest in nuclear energy. Nuclear energy is, in the medium term, the nearest thing to a non-polluting energy source capable of generating power on a large scale we have solar energy is an option, but only on the long term a lot of research and development is required before it can be capable of handling the energy needs of a nation on a sustained basis.

The biggest advantage of nuclear energy is, of course, its non-reliance on oil. Its lack of carbon emission is a well become side benefit. And third generation nuclear reactors minimize the risk of leakage, as the Japanese experience has proven. Give the global electricity consumption is expected to double in the next few decades while oil prices go through the roof, the attitude towards nuclear energy was bound to change. Technological advances are making its use safer more economical.

The 2006 expert committee on energy estimated India's power needs at 990, 00 MW by 2031-32, up from 114000 MW today. This assumed a GDP growth rate of 9% which is very optimistic. But if indeed India grows so fast, coal, hydel and non-conventional energy sources will meet at best 75% of India's needs in 2030, and this proportion will keep declining as coal reserves deplete, then only nuclear energy alone can fill this gap. The gap and India's need for nuclear energy will keep rising in future decades.

Through the Indo-us nuclear deal the agreement is between the two states possessing advanced nuclear technology, both the parties having the same benefits and advantages. The purpose of the agreement is to enable full civil nuclear energy cooperation between India and the United States. The agreement provides full civil nuclear energy cooperation covering nuclear reactors and aspects of the associated nuclear fuel cycle including environment and reprocessing. This agreement would help to address the problem of energy deficit that has emerged as one of the primary constraints an accelerating India's growth rate. Presently, only 3% of India's energy needs are met from nuclear sources. India plans to produce 20,000 MWE from the nuclear sector by 2020 an increase from the current 3,700 MWE.

Of crucial interest to India are articles 2,4,5,6 and 14 of the agreement. Defining the scope of cooperation, article 2 allows advance nuclear research and development (R&D) and the setting up of a reserve stockpile of nuclear fuel to guard against any disruption of supply during the life time of the reactors it also affirms that the agreement will not affect any military nuclear activities and the three stage nuclear programme, the next clause set out the field covered by the agreement which include exchange of information on research in controlled thermo nuclear experimental reactor project of which India is member.

The agreement does not hinder India's military nuclear programme and provides for uninterrupted supply of fuel. If the fuel supplies are disrupted, the US will convene a meeting of supplier countries including Russia, France and United Kingdom to take steps to restore the supply.

The increased share of nuclear power in India energy will diminish the reliance on fossil fuels and reduce commissioner of carbon dioxide (CO_2) from India, through this agreement will set the stage to end India's isolation from world commerce in nuclear technology for over three decades.

Nuclear Deal an Assessment

The agreement has 17 articles which deals with definitions, scope of protection, transfer of information, nuclear trade, transfer of nuclear material, non-nuclear material, equipment, components and related technology, nuclear fuel cycle activities, storage and retransfer of physical protection peaceful use, IAEA safeguards environmental protection, implementation of the agreement consultations, termination and cessation of cooperation, settlement of disputes, entry into force and duration, and administrative arrangements. The agreement stipulates that such cooperation will include nuclear reactors and aspects of the associated nuclear fuel cycle, including technology transfer an industrial or commercial scale. It would also include development of a strategic reserve of nuclear fuel to guard against any disruption of supply over the life time of our reactors. The US has a longstanding policy of not supplying to any country enrichment, reprocessing and heavy water production facilities. This agreement provides for such transfers to India only through an amendment.

The ambit of the deal includes research, development, design, construction, operation, maintenance and use of nuclear reactors, reactor experiments and decommissioning. The US will have the right to seek return of nuclear fuel and technology but it will compensate for the costs incurred as a consequence of such removal. India can develop a strategic reserve of nuclear fuel to guard against any disruption of supply over the life time of its reactors. The agreement provides for consultation the circumstances, including changed security environment before termination of the nuclear cooperation. There is a provision for one year notice period before termination of the agreement. The US is to engage the NSG to help India obtain full access to the international fuel market, including reliable uninterrupted and continual access to fuel supplies from in several nations.

Some important questions arises from the whole issue. Could a country follow an independent foreign policy to achieve its national interest in the current globalised era when it is bound by international and bilateral agreements? What would be the Pro and cons. If India back track from this agreement? In order to ensure free and fair IAEA inspections civilian nuclear facilities and to be repeated from the military related ones. There is concern in same quarters about the US Bill that seeks "fall back" inspections of the IAEA concludes that it is unable to carry out proper inspection because India is not cooperating. In such occasions, India has to permit bilateral inspections.

The US diplomatically pressurized the Indian government to under take the following measures to reach full civil nuclear energy cooperation. First of all, India has to separated civilian nuclear facilities, and then India needs facilities and accept IAEA safeguards on separated civilian nuclear facilities. Then India needs to sign an additional protocol for the supervision of nuclear facilities by the IAEA. Besides, India has to support US efforts for a multilateral fissile Material cut off treaty (FMCT). India can not transfer enrichment and reprocessing technologies to other state. Finally, India is to advert to NSG guide lines and Missile technology control Regime (MTCR) on civilian nuclear facilities in perpetuity to secure nuclear materials and technology from being transferred to other states. In response to apprehensions as regards how the legislation would make an impact on India, Pranab Mukherjee, the external Affairs Minister made a statement in the Indian parliament.

The left parties aired their concern on the nuclear deal in a statement saying that the deal has direct implications for national interest and sovereignty as it curtails India's Independent foreign policy. Therefore, they objected to the operatinalisation of the deal. The central government sought to allay the left's concerns about the Indo-Us nuclear deal by saying that India was not bound by the Hyde Act.

The two contentious agreements related to indo-US Nuclear Deal are the 123 Agreement and the Hyde Act. The Hyde Act which is originally known as 'Henry J. Hyde united states. India peaceful Atomic energy cooperation Act of 2006. States that secure India's full and active participation in United States efforts to dissuade isolate and if necessary sanction and contain Iran for its efforts to acquire weapons of mass destruction.

On 27 September, the House of Representations cleared the Indo-US nuclear deal as 298 members favored the Bill while 117 voted against on 1 October; Senate approved the Indo-US civil nuclear deal with 86 votes for the 13 against. The following day, US Secretary of states Condoleza Rice visited.

New Delhi to sign the nuclear agreement but New Delhi insisted that it would do so only after president Bush signs in into a law. President Bush signed legislative bill to law on October 8 2008. The law is known as United States India nuclear cooperation approval and non proliferation enhancement Act. India's external Affairs Minster Mr. Pranab Mukherjee visited US an 10th October 2008 and singed the final document with US secretary of state Condoleza Rice.

REFERENCES

1. Daniel Yergin 2006, "Ensuring Energy Security" Foreign affairs 2006 vol.85 No.2 pp 69.

2. India Joins Nuclear club gets NSG waiver (www.ndtv.com)

3. Shahi R.V, "India's strategy towards energy development and energy security. Secretary to the government of India.

4. IAEA board approves India safeguards agreement 2008

5. .Kapur,K.D., Nuclear Non Proliferation Diplomacy: Nuclear power program in the third world. New Delhi London publishers 1993

6. .Mahapatra, Chintamani ,Indo-Us Relations into the 21st century New Delhi 1997.

7. Gangadhara,R.Sastry, Indo-US Nuclear deal: A Preliminary assessment Third Concept May 2006.

8. Sultan, Adil Mohammad., Indo-Us Civilian Nuclear Cooperation Agreement; Implication on South Asian Security Environment. Stimson Center July 2006.

9. Bharadwaj, Anshu, India's future electric power requirements and role of nuclear energy. Economic and Political Weekly March 25, 2009.

10. Ayoob, Mohammad, The Third World security predicament: state making regional conflict, and the

international system boulder, London: Lancer publisher, 1996.

11. Sawin, L. janet and stair peter. Cultivating Renewable alternative to oil. State of World, 2006.

BIBLIOGRAPHY

Ahmad, Talmid. Oil diplomacy for India's security foreign service institute new delhi 2007.

Altas, syed farid, Alternative Discourses in Asian social, National University of Singapore 2006.

Ayoob, Mohammed, The Third world security predicament; state making regional conflict, and the international system boulder, London: lynne publisher, 1996.

Bajpai, U.S India security: The political- strategic Environment New Delhi, Lancer publishers, 1982.

Bajpai, Kant and matto Amitabh., Engaged Democracies: Indo-US Relation in the 21st century New Delhi 2000.

Ballan, Vishwa, Governance of water Xavier labour relations institute (XLRI) Jamshad pure 2008.

Baylis, john and steve smith, The Globilization of world politics. An introduction to international relations. Oxford university press 2001.

Beck, U., Risk Society: towards a new modernity London sage 1992.

Beaton, Lenonard, A reform of power: A proposal for an International security system, London 1972.

Bhambhari, C.P., The Foreign Policy of India, New Dehli sterling 1987.

Buzan, Barry & Lene House, international security, London school of economics and political science university of correnphagan 2007.

Chellany, Brahma, nuclear proliferation: the US India conflict, New Delhi; orient lengman ltd 1993.

Chopra, Ashwami Kumar., India's policy on disarmament. New Delhi ABC publishers 1984.

Choudhary, Kameslhwer., Globilization, governance reforms and development in india kalinga institute of industrial technology bhudanswer 2007.

Choudhary,parvein, k., the united state and india state university of New York 2008.

Choudhary, S.R., Nuclear Politics New Delhi press 2006.

Chris,smith. Light weapons and ethnic conflict in south Asia Cambridge 1995.

Clegg, stewart., power and organization university of technology Sydaney 2006.

Compbell, D.,writing security, Manchester University press 1992.

Cohen, Stephan p. and park, the security of south Asia: American and Indian perspective New Delhi Vstaar publisher 1988.

Deudney, D.,the case against linking environmental degradation and national security Millennium press 1991.

Dighe, shared. Democracy and social change share publishing house New Delhi 1997.

Dutt V,P., India and the world New Dehli, sanchar publication 1990.

Dutt. V.P., India's foreign policy in changing world New Delhi Vikas publishing house 1999.

Flaviw, christoper., china india and new world order state of world 2006.

Gawdat, baghat., central Asia and Energy Security aslant affairs 2006.

Gibbs, Erin and Brunschot Van, Risk Balance and Security Rutgers University 2007.

Gorden, sanday., india's rice to power in the twentieth century and beyond , London Macmillian 1995.

Hastedt, gllenn P, The American foreign policy prentice Hale New jersey, 2008.

Herz, J., Idealistic International and the security dilemma World politic 1950.

Howard, B., Schaffer, Bowless,: New dealer in the cold war New Dehli 1994.

Hussain., Monirul., interrogating development Guwahati University press 2008.

Brands, H.W., India and the United States. The cold peace Boston 1990.

Jawhari, R.C., American Diplomacy and indepence for india Vora and company, 1970.

Jetly Nency., India's foreign policy: challenges and prospects New Delhi. Vikas publishing house 1999.

Kamath, P.M., Indo-US Relations Dynamics of change. South Asian publisher New Delhi 1987.

Kamath P.M., The Relevance of American election to India Free press journal London 1904.

Kamath M.V., The United states and india 1967-76 Washington D.C. 1976.

Kapur, Ashok., India's Nuclear option: Atomic Diplomacy Decision Making New York praeger 1979.

Kapur, K.D., Nuclear Non Proliferation Diplomacy: Nuclear power program in the third world. Delhi London publisher 1993.

Kaushik, surendranath, India and the south Asia New Delhi south Asia publisher 1987.

k. subrahmannyan., Security beyond survival, P.R. Kumara swamy J.N.U. New Delhi 2004.

Kolthera, verghase., Society, State and Security vice admiral Navy 1999.

Larson, A Jeffery, Arms control viva books private limited New Delhi 2007.

Laster, R. Brown, Challenges of the new century L.R. & B 2000.

Limyae, S.P., U.S. Indian Relations the pursuit of Accommodation Boulder, colarado westview, cliffs 1999.

Lt. gen. kathpalia, P.N. National security perspective New Delhi lancer international 1986.

Mahapatra, chintamani, Indo-US Relations into 21th century New Delhi 1997.

Man singh, surjit. S., India's search for power, Indra Gandhi's foreign policy 1966-82 New Delhi sage publisher 1984.

Mashra, S.K & Puri V.K., Indian economy part iv Himalaya public house 2007.

Michal, Ranner., Fighting for Survival, Environmental Decline, social conflict and the new age of insecurity New York 1986.

Morgenthau, H. J., Politics among nations the struggle for power and peace New York Alford Knopt 1978.

Mellor, John W., India: A Rising middle power New Delhi select service syndicate 1981.

Mohite, Dilip, H., Indo-US Relations: Issues in conflict & cooperation New Delhi south Asian publisher 1995.

M.S.Rajan, India's forign policy and relations New Delhi 1998.

Narayanan, K.R., India & America; Essay in understanding New Delhi: dialogue publisher 1984.

Nayer, Balder, Raj. American Geo-politics and India, New Delhi 1976.

Norman, D. Palmar., The United States and India. The dimension of influence New York 1984.

Ouapally, Deppa., Nuclear cooperation: Challenges and cooperation Banglore; National Institute of Advanced Studies 1997.

Pant, K.C. ,Philosophy of our defense. Lancer international New Delhi 1989.

Paranjape, Srikant., U.S Non proliferation policy in action; South Asia New Delhi: Strelling Publishers 2007.

Parkovleh, Geroge., India's Nuclear Bomb: The impact on global proliferation New Delhi Oxford University Press 2000.

Poulose, T.T. ed, Perspective of India's Nuclear Policy. New Delhi Young Asia publishers 1978.

Poulose, T.T. ed,. The CTBT and the Rise of Nuclear nationalism in India, New Delhi Lancer book 1996.

Quester, George. H., The Nuclear Weapons State , Journal of Conflict Resolution 1983.

Raju, J.C. Thamas, The great power triangle and Asian Security , Laxington 1983.

Rana, A.P. ed, Four Decades of Indo-U.S Relations: A Commemorative retrospective, New Delhi Haranand publication 1994.

Restoge, Maharaj, Krishna. The New Asian Power Dynamics National Security Board New Delhi 2007.

Robert, F. Goheen., Indo-US Relations: Nuclear Proliferation and technology transfer, New Delhi 1984.

Rose, James N, ed, World Politics: An Introduction London, 1976.

R.C. Jha., international security of a democratic state.

Rudolph, Liyod and Susanne, ed. The regional imperative. US Foreign Policy towards South Asian State, New Jersey: Atlantic High Lands 1981.

Sawin, L. Janet and Stair Peter. Cultivating Renewable alternative to oil, State of World 2006.

Sharma, P.D., Ecology and Environment, Restoogi publication New Delhi 2008.

Sharma, R, India and Emerging Asia J.N.U Calcutta research 2005.

Singh, Jasjit, ed., Nuclear India New Delhi 1999.

Singh, Jasjit, ed., Indo- US Relations in a changing world, New Delhi Lancer international and IDSA 1992.

Singh Nauninal, India A Rising Power, Authors press global network New Delhi 2006.

Singh, Surahali, Ajet. India's Security in resurgent, Asia publication New opportunities. Delhi 1997.

Singh Atisha and Mehta Modhip, Indian Foreign Policy Challenges and Opportunities. Foreign Service Institute New Delhi 2008.

Spector, Leonard. S., Nuclear Proliferation: The Spread Of Nuclear Weapons, New York 1984.

Spector, Leonard, S., Nuclear Proliferation: today New York vintage Books 1984.

Subrahmanyam, K., India and the nuclear challenges, New Delhi Lancer International and IDSA 1986.

Sultan, Tanvir. Indo- US Relations: A Study of Foreign policies, New Delhi Deep and Deep publishers 1983.

S.D. Muni., The Emerging Cold War in Asia: India's options strategic Analysis, New Delhi 1997.

Thomas, Raju, G.C. India's Nuclear security, Marquetee university 2000.

Thomas, S. Tough., Peaceful Nuclear Explosions and disarmament, peace research review 1960.

Thickner, J.A., Revisioning Security, Cambridge Policy press 1995.

Tihamas, Wesis, The United Nations and Changing World Politics Western press 1997.

Vinod, M.S., United States Foreign Policy Towards India: A Diagnosis of the American approach, New Delhi lancer books 1991.

Tiwari, S.C., Indo-US Relations 1947-76, New Delhi Lancer books, 1991.

Watt. S., The Renaissance of security studies , international studies 1991.

Watt, Z.K., Man the state and war, New York Columbia University press 1999.

Walter, Sinnotl and B. Richard., perspective on climate changes, science economics, politics Ethics Horvath JA press 2005.

Wendt, A., Bridgining the theory meta theory gap in international relations 1991.

William, T. Tan., Asia emerging regional order, Tokyo 2000.

W. Kuch, Gert., Democracy Diversity, Stability, published by Jajiv Beri Macmillian New Delhi 2002.

Ya daran leela, U.S- Pakistan Relations (kurukshetra, kurukhastra university press 1979.

www.ingramcontent.com/pod-product-compliance
Lightning Source LLC
Chambersburg PA
CBHW070558290526
45790CB00002B/730